Acknowledgements

A great many contractors spent time visiting with me about common problems that arise with their customers. It is their goal, I find, to help their customers in any way they can. "Information passed on helps our customers financially and enables us to better communicate. In this way we better serve them and are more efficient..." as stated by a local technician/owner. I thank all of you for your time, insight and assistance in this endeavor.

A special thanks to Jim Geraci for his time and effort as a model for the cover of this book. Although some may think the cover is not tasteful, our model is a true gentleman and I applaud his hootspa.

Stop that Crack!
Easy Household Fixes

ISBN 978-0-9825793-5-0

Times are hard and we must go beyond the norm to save money. This guide is designed for just that. There is no need to pay for a technician when we can DO IT OURSELVES! We work too hard for our money. Many of the things we call a professional for can be done ourselves for little or no cost. A quick inspection, knowing what to look for, can curtail huge problems later.

Here are some of the things you need to navigate this book:

Watch for the following icons as they will indicate helpful information and warnings.

Some are listed as easy -

Some are listed as somewhat easy -

Some are listed as difficult but doable -

Some actions may require special knowledge -

Watch for moving parts -

Check the owners guide before beginning -

Specific tools may be required -

Disconnect power before proceeding -

Maintenance can be scheduled -

A lack of information costs home owners thousands of dollars each year. It is our intent to give you enough information about maintaining your home to recoup at least one service call per year. Most maintenance of simple systems can easily be performed by anyone with very basic tools and in many cases no tools at all.

If you prevent one service call by using information from this book, you have paid for the book and a night out on the town!

Contents

BUILDING ENVELOPE

YOUR WINDOWS

ALUMINUM FRAMED WINDOWS

Over time the aluminum frames of your windows may oxidize or the springs that make opening a window effortless may begin to bind. Cleaning your windows and protecting the parts from the elements will add life to the windows.

☻ Clean the exterior portions of your aluminum windows with a powdered laundry detergent and water. Use a soft brush to loosen solids in the sash and tracks. Use a vacuum cleaner wand that will fit into these areas to remove loose materials when dry. Lubricate aluminum slides with a silicone lubricant. Oils will catch and hold dust, binding the slides over time. Silicone will apply dry and reduces the amount of grit that might stick in place. Steel springs and thumb latches on the inside of the window should be lubricated with penetrating oil. A good car wax applied to the aluminum trim will help prevent oxidation.

📅 Maintain your aluminum windows every time you clean them; but never less than twice per year.

WOODEN WINDOWS

Wood windows are time proven to be not only highly efficient but add a nice look to your home. Proper inspection and maintenance is a must.

Inspect your wood windows every time you clean them. Look for signs of rotted wood, chipped or peeling paint and loose or missing caulk. If signs of rot are found, replace the wood if possible. Never paint over rotted wood as it will continue unseen. Keeping the windows painted is the best defense against deterioration. Therefore, at the first sign of chipped or peeling paint, scrape sand and repaint the wood surfaces. The interior of your windows will normally only need to be repainted when the room is repainted. Where glass panes are set into the wood frames, caulk is used to seal water and air out. Take care to not damage adjacent paint when you caulk. Use a furniture wax to lubricate wood on wood sliders.

Inspect your wood windows frequently. Maintain immediately as needed. Repaint or varnish the exterior every two to five years. Rotted wood will feel spongy or soft when prodded with a screwdriver.

VINYL WINDOWS

With vinyl windows it's more about what not to do than what should be done. When cleaning your vinyl windows, take care not to use any cleaner that has an abrasive or solvent. Even a mild abrasive will have an effect on how the finish will look. Always check the weep holes located on the bottom outside and make sure they are not blocked.

YOUR DOORS

😎 Moisture is the leading enemy of wood exterior doors. If the surface feels rough to the touch or cracks can be seen; if the clear coat appears hazy or has lost its shine, the door may need to be refinished. If the wood door begins to stick when humidity increases, check the edges and top of the door to make sure they are sealed.

YOUR DOOR HARDWARE

😎 Locksmiths are often called out to remove a key stuck in a deadbolt. Do not procrastinate when the key has to be wiggled around to get it in and out. Use compressed air such as one would use to clean a computer key board and blow out the key hole to remove any particles lodged in side. Take care to protect your eyes. Use graphite lubricant (available at most stores where keys are made) to lubricate the key hole. Follow package directions, it's a snap.

😎 When the latch or lock no longer latches in place, check the following items. Open the door and inspect the hinge screws. If they loosen, the door may drop down and the latches will not align with the striker plate. Next, examine the striker plate to confirm the striker plate screws are tight and the throat is not blocked. In wood, match sticks or tooth picks can be used to fill in worn screw holes and the screws can be reinserted.

😎 Frozen locks can be thawed by heating the key and inserting the key slowly into the key hole. Use gloves to handle the hot key and repeat as often as needed to get it working again. Keeping the lock well lubricated will normally prevent lock freeze up as the lubricant will displace the water.

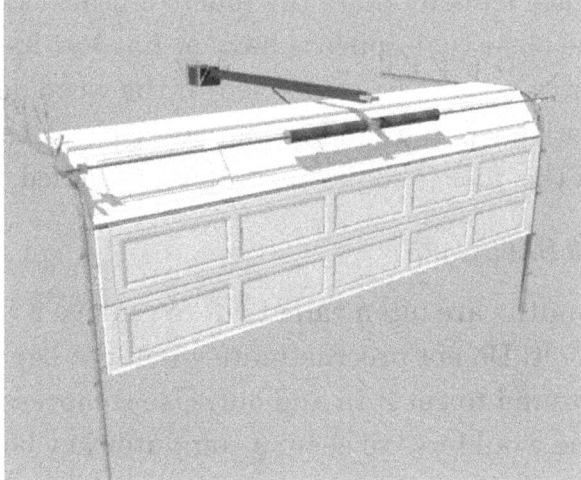

GARAGE DOORS

☺ Many types of garage doors are in service today. They are subjected to wind loads equal to your walls. If your garage door is wood, keep it painted or varnished to prevent decay or warping. All surfaces should be sealed including the edges.

All moving parts such as rollers, hinges and swing pins should be lubricated with penetrating oil. ⚙ Take care to keep the door locked into place when examining or lubricating moving parts. Metal on metal sliding parts should be lubricated with a silicon lubricant unless your owner's manual instructs otherwise. Inspect for loose bolts and tighten as needed. ❗ NEVER try to adjust springs on a garage door. Always have this service performed by trained personnel.

📅 Lubrication, adjustments and bolt tightening should be performed once a year. Painting wood doors should normally occur every two to five years.

YOUR INSULATION

The separation between you and the temperature outside is maintained primarily by your insulation. The porous material forces the movement of heat to slow to a crawl. Heat travels in and around the natural barriers of uncompressed insulation and it's resistance to the flow is measured in R-value. When the insulation material becomes compressed, whether by gravity or poor installation practices, the R-value diminishes dramatically.

☺ The R-value of insulation can be calculated by a free computer program provided by the U. S. Energy Department. Go to http://www.energycodes.gov/rescheck/download.stm to download it. It will also help you choose proper energy efficient replacement windows by giving you the recommended values. This program is designed for home builders, but with a little common sense it can guide you a long way. If you have questions, contact your local building official and ask what the "default R-values" are.

📅 If your attic insulation has settled more than 25%, then it has lost most of its value.

YOUR ATTIC FANS, TURBINES & VENTS

MOTORS

Electric motor powered fans usually have a belt. This belt will stretch with age. If the belt has become cracked this is an indication it will fail soon and should be replaced. On many of the old attic fans, the motor will slide on a bracket to loosen and tighten the belt. Make sure the power is off. Loosen the bolts holding the motor in place. Slide the motor on the bracket slots tightening the belt after it is replaced. Tighten the bolts. The belt is tight when it has about an inch of deflection with light pressure. Make sure the motor is not setting at an angle to the fan pulley. A straight edge placed against the pulleys will help with alignment. To get a replacement belt, take the old one to an auto parts store. They have a tool to measure it even if the numbers have long since faded.

🙂 Oiling a motor will increase its life and save a very expensive service call. Some of the newer motors do not have oil ports. If the motor can be lubricated, it will have a small rubber or plastic plugs located above the bushings. Pull the plugs out and drip a few drops of machine oil down the holes. Replace the plugs.

📅 Service electric motors and inspect belts once a year and tighten or replace belts as needed.

TURBINES

Unpowered roof turbines are used to move air through the attic space. This helps to remove moisture from the space and in some areas, excess heat. Most of the newer models have sealed bearings and will not require much maintenance. Inspect your turbine for debris from trees and birds. Verify that dust or grit is not binding the lower track. Oiling the bearing on top with machine oil and using graphite lubricant on the bottom will help keep it in tip top shape. In areas where the turbine will be covered with snow in the winter, it is prudent to bag it with a couple of heavy duty garbage bags and duct tape them in place. Remove snow from around them as soon as possible. In regions where snow will not cover them, but you don't want the warm air sucked out; a homemade Styrofoam plug can be inserted from the bottom to keep you off the roof.

BASEMENT

YOUR BASEMENT SUMP

Keeping your basement dry is the key to longevity.
Moisture in the ground will run down the outside of your
basement walls and eventually make its way through any
crack or unsealed portion of a wall or the floor. Water that
cannot be sealed out is removed by drain systems.

The most common drain system is a sump pump.
Open the pit where the sump pump is located and make
sure the inlet screen is clean. Pour a bucket of water into
the pit; just enough to raise the float and activate the
pump. If the pump does not activate, check to make sure
the power cord is plugged it and the ground fault circuit
interrupter (GFCI) is not tripped (if so equipped). If it still
doesn't work, a technician may need to be called before
the heavy rains begin. Replace the grate when
maintenance is complete.

This maintenance should be performed four times a
year and coordinated to occur before rainy seasons and/or
snow melts.

Disconnect the power to the sump pump. Remove
the pump from the pit and clean both the pump and the
pit. Using the owner's manual, locate and lubricate
the motor bearings. Reset the pump into the pit;
reconnect the power and test the system by pouring water
into the pit until the pump activates. It is important to
make a special effort to keep the float actuator clear of the
side of the pit. It must be able to move freely.

12

This maintenance should be performed at least once each year.

MECHANICAL SYSTEMS

YOUR CENTRAL COOLING SYSTEM

The most common central air and heat systems are also known as a split system. The portion of the system inside the home, called an evaporator, collects heat and moves it outside to the condenser and releases the heat outside. For heat, the inside unit is combined with a furnace or electric heat strips. The evaporator and the condenser appear to be large appliances that stand alone, hence the reference, split system. The two appliances are actually one system and must be matched for proper function.

A similar system known as a heat pump can be reversed and pump heat from the outside. This unit also uses heat strips, but they assist the heat pump to increase efficiency.

If you're A/C system stops running and you can't get it to restart, here are some things to check before you call a technician:

- Check the breakers and verify a breaker isn't tripped.
- Check to see if the emergency drain pan located under the evaporator (the inside unit) is full of water. A float switch may be on the side of the pan. It is designed to shut off the system if the primary condensate drain stops up. Push the float down to verify this is your problem. If so, wet-vac the water out of the pan and refer to the *Your Condensate Drain* section below to unstop the primary drain.

14

Your A/C System

The key to an efficient cooling system is cleanliness. The system uses a coolant to remove heat and moisture from the air in your home. This is done by air circulating through coils with fins placed close together to allow transfer of heat by contact. When these fins become clogged with dust, mold or other unseen particles, the ability to properly operate is reduced.

The first line of defense is your air filter. Choose a good quality filter that properly fits the filter frame. A corrugated filter has a large surface area which works well and helps to reduce noise. Horsehair or fiber filter catches the least amount of small clogging particles. Some of the more expensive filters are very efficient as long as they're kept clean.

Replace or clean your air filter once a month minimum. Some dusty or humid environments may require replacement more often.

Your Condenser

Your condenser coils (outside) must be kept clean as they use outside air to remove heat. A switch or disconnect next to the unit must be disengaged. Using a water hose, spray through the open top into the coils flushing out all debris and dirt. Then move to the outside of the unit and spray downward to wash the debris down and off the coils. Engage the switch or disconnect upon completion.

While cleaning the coils, inspect for closed fins that may have been bent over from an impact. A special tool called a coil fin comb can be used to straighten the bent fins in most cases. This will help to maintain efficiency.

NOTE – Never mow the grass next to your condenser while it is running as the grass may be pulled into the coils clogging them. In the southern regions of the United States it is important to treat for fire ants around your condenser. They love to get into the electrical system and clog up the contactors. This was the most common service call on the gulf coast according to a recent poll.

Washing the condenser coils should occur twice a year. Wash them once at the beginning of the warm season and once in the middle part of the warm season.

YOUR EVAPORATOR

Your evaporator coils will eventually need to be cleaned as well. Turn power off to the system. Open the housing where the evaporator coil is located. It will normally be either a slab coil or a V shaped coil. Under the bottom of the coil will be a pan designed to catch condensation and remove it to a drain. Using a 50/50 bleach/water solution in a spray bottle, thoroughly soak the coil. Use a soft bristled brush to remove the "gunk" from the coil. Pour the remaining bleach/water solution into the pan so it will remove any slime build up in the condensate drain line.

Caution – While using a bleach solution protect your eyes and clothes. There are coil cleaning products available on the market that work very well. Do not use vinegar based cleaners as they may have a chemical reaction with the aluminum coil fins.

📅 Cleaning the evaporator coils once a year at the beginning of the warm season is recommended for the best efficiency.

YOUR CONDENSATE DRAINS

A central system usually has a condensate drain from the pan below the evaporator coils to a drain and a secondary drain system that may terminate over an outside window or even over a bath tub. If you observe water dripping out over the window or in the bath tub then your primary drain may be clogged.

🙂 To unclog the primary drain, locate the evaporator coil and the pan below the coil. The pan may be integrated into the system or located separately below the unit. The primary drain may connect directly to the unit with a secondary pan below the unit. If the secondary pan has water in it, the primary drain is probably clogged. Disconnect the primary drain line and use compressed air to blow out the primary drain line. A cup of bleach water poured down the primary drain will maintain the drain from slime accumulation.

📅 Unclog the line as needed. To maintain the line clog free, pour a cup of bleach down the line twice per warm season.

YOUR FURNACE

GAS FIRED

Maintaining a gas fired furnace will extend its life as well as maintain its efficiency. It could be natural gas or propane, they work the same.

Shut off power to the furnace. Turn the gas off to the unit. Open the housing where the blower motor is located. With the soft brush attachment on your vacuum, remove all dust from within this area and on the motor. Some areas may need to be wiped with a damp cloth. Check the blower motor for oil ports. Oil ports will be located over the shaft at each end of the motor. Some motors are permanently sealed and do not have them. If your motor does have oil ports, open the oil port and put ten to twenty drops of machine oil in and reclose them. Inspect the belt(s) for wear, cracks and looseness. Replace or tighten if needed. Replace filter. Turn gas and electricity back on. Observe pilot light. The flame should be blue with an occasional streak of yellow. The center of the flame should be blue green. If the flame does not look right, call a technician because the air/gas mixture needs to be adjusted.

Note – The heat exchanger on gas fired and oil fired furnaces should be inspected by qualified personnel. Recognizing deficiencies in heat exchangers takes experience and specialized training.

Service your furnace blower compartment at least once per year. Change your filter at least once a month.

18

YOUR DUCT SYSTEM

Attic ducts and below floor ducts basically are the same. The biggest concern with duct work is whether they leak and if they are properly insulated.

🙂 Enter the crawl space or attic where your duct work is located. Move your hand around the joints of the duct work. Feel for air escaping from the ducts. You may use a piece of tissue paper to visibly see the movement of air.

To repair a duct, it is best to use mastic purchased from an air conditioning and heating supply. Install per the manufacturers installation guide. However, you can use duct tape. When purchasing duct tape, don't use the cheap from the dollar store. Examine the roll and look for the UL listing. The UL181A or UL181B has a different type of adhesive that will not release itself within a year. The aluminum tape should also be UL181 listed. The listed tape will cost more but the savings will be, not having to redo it later.

The duct insulation will have a vinyl or Mylar outer covering. It should have an R-8 insulating value unless it was installed before 2000. One can add insulation over the existing insulation to increase its value.

📅 Check your duct for leaks every two years and after service personnel have been in the crawl spaces or attic.

Your Exhaust Systems

A residence has a great many exhaust systems. The bathing and laundry areas are designed to reduce steam. The toilet room or restroom is exhausted to remove odors. The kitchen is vented to remove cooking steam and odors.

Your Restroom Exhaust Fan

☺ The restroom and laundry room exhaust fan duct should terminate outside the home. The fan itself is normally located in the housing in the room. The cover is usually in place with a friction lock. If you can't find any screws then you're safe to pull down on it. The fan is plugged in inside the housing. The fan assembly normally just snaps in place. Some of them have one or two small screws to hold them in place. Replacing the motor assembly is a snap. Cleaning and oiling the old motor has been known to squeeze another year out of them.

Your Kitchen Vent Hood

☺ Kitchen vent hoods sometimes have a filter that is activated charcoal. Clean this filter or replace it per the manufacturer's service guide. If your vent hood exhausts outside, clean it in accordance with your manufacturer's maintenance guide.

📅 Restroom and laundry room exhaust systems should be serviced as needed. Kitchen filters should be serviced monthly where heavy oily cooking occurs. Vent hood ducts should be cleaned annually depending on cooking habits.

ELECTRICAL SYSTEM

YOUR LIGHTS ARE FLICKERING

COMPACT FLUORESCENT

Before you call an electrician, check to see if the light is on a dimmer. The compact fluorescent bulbs are designed to use full power. A dimmer operated on these types of bulbs can make it flicker, cause damage to the bulb or to the dimmer. Dimmer should be full on or replaced with a switch.

Keep an old incandescent light bulb around just to test your circuits serving compact fluorescents. The plastic block at the bottom of the lamp is a ballast and it can go out or even be defective right out of the box. Note – Compact Fluorescent light bulbs cannot handle heat! So if you use them in warm environments, the heat will greatly reduce their life.

EXTERIOR HIGH INTENSITY DISCHARGE (HID) LIGHTS

Your exterior mercury vapor (red glow) or high pressure sodium (yellow glow) lights may cycle on and off. This usually means the lamp is going bad. Be careful changing these bulbs as they generate a great deal more heat than the average bulb. If the light still cycles after changing the bulb, then the ballast kit may need to be replaced.

The photoelectric cells, on many of these lights, twist lock into place. To test a light that uses a photoelectric cell, simply use black electric tape to cover the aperture and give it five minutes or so to activate.

YOUR BREAKER PANEL

The most common types of panels on modern homes are the breaker type panels. As with any system, there are actions you can take to lengthen the life of your equipment. Some actions require special knowledge and care must be taken. If you are not experienced working with electricity, do not open enclosures.

☻ Exercising your breakers maintains a strong system. Make sure that everyone in the house has their computer backed up and they know the power will be going off. When everyone is ready, simply turn each breaker off and then back on again. On occasion, a defective breaker can be found in this way as it may not reset. If this rarity happens, have the breaker replaced by a qualified electrician.

📅 This maintenance should be performed twice a year.

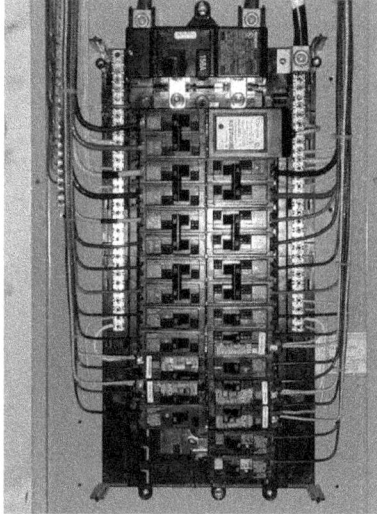

☺ ⚡ Checking connections within panels should be performed by experienced personnel. With the panel cover off and the main power off, use an insulated slot head screwdriver to torque each connection on each breaker, buss bar or fuse blocks. Over time, energy will cause expansion and contraction at these points and the connections will loosen. Loose connections cause heat and failure may eventually occur. Homes with aluminum wiring tend to require this maintenance more often than those with copper wiring.

📅 This maintenance should be performed once every two or three years for homes with copper wiring. Perform this maintenance more often with aluminum wiring.

YOUR DEVICES

A device is the technical term to describe switches and receptacle plugs. As with most electrical equipment, heat is a side effect and an enemy. The use of a device tends to cause heat and this in turn causes metal fatigue or expansion and contraction and loose connections. The circle continues until a failure occurs.

Turn the main power off. Remove a plug face plate. Using a voltage tester, verify no power is present. Even with the main power is turned off; it is possible to have feedback through the system neutral (aka grounded conductor). If no power is present, remove the upper and lower receptacle mounting screws. Pull the outlet out gently and locate the connections on the side. Inspect the wires and the coatings on them. If evidence of overheating is present, remove the damaged portion. Inspect the outlet for heat damage or cracks and replace if damaged. With a slot head screwdriver torque these connections tight. If no damage is observed carefully reinsert the outlet assembly into the box. Take care to keep the outlet in the center portion of the box so the exposed portions of current carrying parts do not come into contact with the box. Reinstall the mounting screws and face plate. Repeat this with each receptacle outlet in the home. The same procedure may be used for switches.

This maintenance should be performed every seven to ten years on homes wired with copper. Homes with aluminum wiring tend to require this maintenance more often than those with copper wiring.

YOUR ELECTRICAL SERVICE

The "service" is the portion of the electrical system where your connection is made to the utility company. Typically, the meter, the main breaker panel, the ground rod, and the wires coming from the power company make up a common service.

If your power comes from overhead lines down to a riser, a simple inspection may save you hundreds of dollars. Look at the trees to see if any limbs may need to be trimmed back. In almost every storm with high winds, a limb crashes down on some one's service drop and destroys perfectly good equipment. The power is off, sometimes for days and the repair bill is enormous.

This inspection should be performed at least once a year depending on your trees.

The ground rod and its associated parts are the most important part of your electrical system. It is the safety device that silently stands by guarding every electrical appliance, device and enclosure in your home. Everything electrical, or subject to become energized, MUST be connected to it for your safety. A simple inspection could not only save you a service call, but could even save a family members life.

The ground rod (aka grounding electrode) is normally located below your electrical service (meter). It may be a steel pipe, an iron rod (probably copper coated) or a piece of rebar. The ground rod may be buried below the surface of the soil. When you find it, look for a wire connected to it that is usually about the size of a pencil or slightly smaller. It may be bare or it could be coated. The important thing is that it is connected securely to the rod or pipe. Grasp the rod and twist it. If it moves, this is a sign that it may have rotted off and must be replaced. If the connection is loose on the rod or the wire, tighten it. If it will not tighten, replace the connector. Inspect the wire from the ground up to the point it enters the service enclosure for damage such as may be caused from a weed eater or other physical damage. Have an electrician replace this part as it terminates in a HOT enclosure.

This inspection should occur annually, more if the grounding system is subject to physical damage or if the wire is aluminum.

YOUR STAND-BY GENERATOR

Most stand-by generators utilize an internal combustion engine that turns a generator. The generator provides power to your home, or selected circuits within your home, in case of a power outage. The transfer of power is made by a transfer switch which automatically switches from the utility provider to the generator when the utility's power stops. Note that some stand-by systems use a manual transfer switch.

Most stand-by systems use natural gas or LP gas. This type of fuel does not require much maintenance. Diesel and gasoline may require additives or replacement of fuel. See your owner's manual for this and all maintenance questions.

Shut down your generator in the method the manufacturer describes to prevent the system from activating while you have the housing open. Inspect the engine compartment for oil and fuel leaks. Hoses with cracks should be replaced and connections that have become loose should be tightened. No leaks should be present. Check oil and coolant levels.

Inspect the battery connections. Clean and tighten the connection when needed. If the battery is not one of the maintenance free batteries check the electrolyte levels. Use distilled water to fill to the line on the side of the battery. To check the battery's charge state, a special tool is required. Using a VOLT METER test the voltage between the posts. If the voltage is less than 11 volts, the battery is low. Some digital battery chargers have battery test capabilities. Verify the battery is 90% or better. *Note – The red lead of the volt meter will go to the positive (+) post, and the black lead to the negative (-) post.*

The normal inspection, checking oil and coolant and battery connections should occur once a month. Check the battery state of charge and the electrolyte levels should occur twice a year. Replacement of oil, oil filter, coolant and cleaning or replacement of sparkplugs should occur annually.

PLUMBING SYSTEM

YOUR WATER HEATER

This appliance is the most taken for granted appliance in a typical home today. It is simply expected that hot water will be available for washing everything from ones hands, to dishes, to clothes. A tank type water heater can also be one of the most dangerous systems in a structure. Depending on its energy source, a malfunctioning water heater is capable of electrocution, carbon monoxide poisoning, poisoning from backflow of stagnant water, scalding and explosion. If a replacement is required, a licensed plumber should be used to perform the task and a plumbing inspector should make a safety inspection.

There are some maintenance procedures that can lengthen the life of your water heater and maintain its safety.

ALL TANK TYPE WATER HEATERS

A tank type water heater is the large round tank with water piped to and from it which stores heated water ready for use at all times. This is unlike the tankless type otherwise known as an "On Demand" water heater. All tank type water heaters require a safety device called a "temperature and pressure relief valve" (T&P). It will be located on the top or side within six inches of the top of the tank. It will be brass, shaped in a ninety degree angle and have a small lever on it. This fitting should be piped down and outside or into a drain and possibly just to the floor. When pressures or temperatures within the tank exceed allowable limits this relief valve will release the pressure build up to prevent the tank from superheating the water. This valve must be operated to allow it to open and run water through the relief piping and out. NOTE, the water coming out may be scalding hot and could cause severe burns. If the T&P valve is not piped out or is plugged or missing, call a qualified plumber immediately.

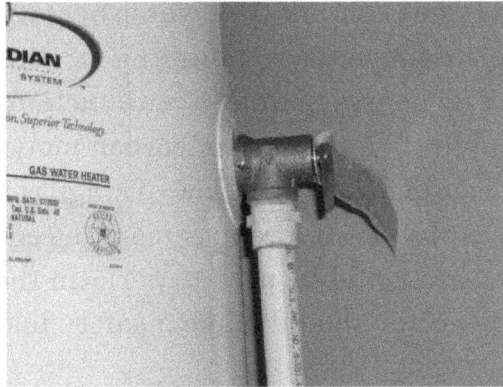

📅 ⓘ *First verify the T&P is piped in a way that hot water will not scald you.* The relief valve should be operated, by lifting the lever, at least twice a year to make sure all water ways are clear. If the valve does not close, it is defective and must be replaced.

YOUR GAS FIRED WATER HEATER

A water heater that uses natural gas or LP gas poses several hazards at one time. All of these hazards can be minimized to a safe point with an inspection and useful information.

😎 The use of fire requires the burning of oxygen. Plenty of air must be provided to any gas fired appliance to prevent it from burning oxygen that your family needs. If the water heater is in a closet, make sure it has air vents from an outside source; such as pipes from the attic or from the crawl space below the home. Check to see these vents are not blocked. In some cases air is used from inside the home. In these cases verify that louvers and vents are not blocked.

☻ Carbon monoxide is also a concern with gas fired appliances. The flue that conducts this harmful exhaust gas must run continuously to the outside of the home with as little horizontal piping as possible. The shorter this pipe is, the less chance something will fall against it and ignite a fire. Verify that the exhaust flue is connected to the "draft hood" (small dome shaped cap on the top of the water heater), extends through the ceiling (through the fire stop, a metal plate that holds the pipe in the center of a hole), through the attic and out of the roof uninterrupted.

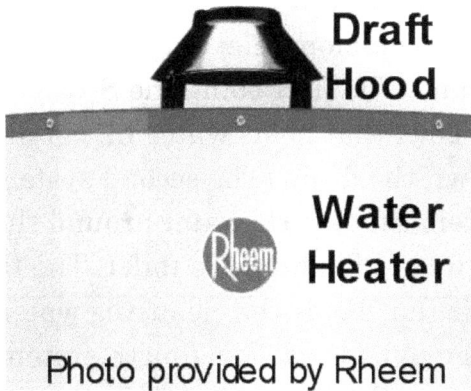

Draft Hood

Water Heater

Photo provided by Rheem

Make sure that the entire pipe is at least one inch or more from any material that isn't stone or metal. Inspect the flue vent termination cap on the roof to confirm the cap is in place and above the snow line. Test the carbon monoxide detector per the manufacturer's guide lines.

Note - A carbon monoxide detector is always a worthwhile investment!

Note – Never store flammable materials in a closet used for a gas fired appliance.

This inspection should occur twice a year and after anything is moved to the attic for storage and after re-roofing.

YOUR ELECTRIC WATER HEATER STOPPED WORKING
Before you call a plumber check the circuit breaker. A normal electric water heater will use a double pole breaker. It will be like two breakers with the levers connected together. Turn it off and then back on again. This one act may save you a service call.

YOUR TOILET

You wouldn't think that a toilet would be as complicated as it can be. The common toilet is a combination of four different systems. The first being the S-trap, which is the portion of the bowl that holds water in, not allowing it from going down the drain. The second system is the cleansing system that swirls water around the bowl removing waste and flushing the toilet. The third system is the reservoir that holds the cleansing water until you decide it is time to be used. The fourth system is the ballcock that controls the amount of water stored in the reservoir and prevents used water from entering your drinking water. Due to this complex array of systems, it is better to maintain your toilet in a reactive manner rather than a proactive manner. View the following list of symptoms and address the symptom with the attached cure.

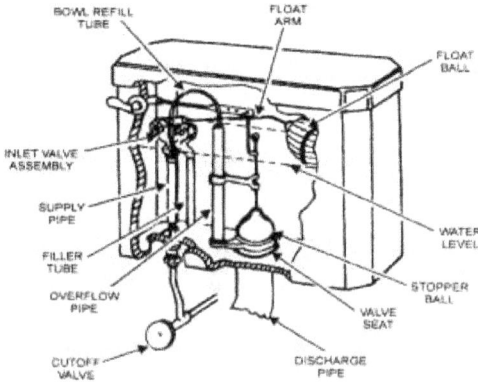

Toilet continuously runs.

🙂 This is a sign the ballcock valve is not seating and closing. Sometimes the float can be adjusted to close the valve. If this does not work, replace the ballcock.

Toilet runs when no one has flushed it.

😎 The flapper is allowing the water in the tank to slowly run into the bowl and down the drain. When the float reaches the low water level, it opens and refills the tank. Replace the flapper to stop this annoying and wasteful symptom.

Toilet seems to take forever to refill.

🙂 This is caused by water running slow. If the area has low water pressure or your home has clogged lines, an easy fix may not be available. Turn the water off at the supply valve usually at the wall. Disconnect the supply line to the tank. Slowly turn the valve on with the hose in a bucket. If the water pressure is high, the problem is probably in the ballcock.

The toilet will not flush when the handle is operated.

☻ The handle connects to a chain (or other apparatus) connecting to the flapper. Verify the chain is short enough to raise the flapper when the handle is operated. It may have become unhooked or broke and may need to be replaced.

The handle must be rattled to stop the toilet from flushing continuously.

☻ Verify that the chain to the flapper isn't too short, or excess chain may be hanging down and preventing the flapper from seating properly. Make sure a foreign object isn't lodged under the flapper. Check the handle to verify the nut hasn't backed off binding the arm preventing it from dropping down. *Note - The nut on the handle has a left hand thread.*

The toilet doesn't flush.

☻ This is normally a stoppage and may be pushed on through with a plunger. In some cases a closet auger may be required. If you use a closet auger, read the use instructions to prevent damage to the porcelain in the bowl.

Water leaks out from under the bowl or a sewer smell is in the bathroom.

☺ This could occur if the wax seal is damaged. If the toilet is not firmly secured down the wax seal will eventually fail. When the seal is replaced make sure the bowl is shimmed in place and grouted down.

Water is dripping from the toilet tank.

☺ There are four places the water could be coming from. The first place to check is where the supply line connects to the ballcock. The nut above this connection holds the ballcock in the tank and is sealed with a rubber washer. Try tightening this first. The second place is where the tank connects to the bowl. Two bolts hold the tank on to the bowl which use rubber washers as seals, and a large soft gasket that seals the water connection between the tank and the bowl. Be careful not to over tighten these bolts and break the porcelain. The third might be the tank has a crack. This might occur if warm water is run into a cold tank. The tank may be creating condensation due to cold water entering the warm house. In this case you can insulate the tank to stop the condensation. Remember when chasing a leak that water will follow the contour of the toilet and following it back can be tricky.

The seat is loose.

☺ The seat is attached to the bowl with two plastic bolts. The bolt heads are covered with caps on the hinge and can be exposed by popping the cap up with a slot head screw driver. The nuts on the bottom are designed to be held with your fingers, so no special tools are needed.

Blue Water comes out of faucets.

If you have blue water coming out of your faucet or in your ice, do not drink it. Check your toilet and verify that the ballcock valve is above the water line. If the ballcock valve is above the water line, and you have blue water, call the water purveyor immediately as this is an indication that water has flowed backward from someone's toilet into the drinking water.

YOUR TUB AND SHOWER

Fiberglass tubs and showers sometimes present a challenge to keep clean. The neat thing is, the fiberglass used, is not unlike that of an automobile. After cleaning your fiberglass, simply apply some good car wax per the package instructions to keep your bath easily cleanable for longer periods of time. How often you perform this task depends on hardness of water and bathing habits.

YOUR FAUCETS

YOUR FAUCET SUDDENLY STOPPED WORKING
First verify whether the hot or the cold or both of them stopped running. If both the hot and cold has stopped running, check the aerator. When work has been performed on the water line, rust or other particulates flow downstream and may stop up your aerator. The aerator is screwed onto or into the outlet of the faucet.

If either one of the hot or the cold has stopped and not the other, the most common problem will be in the valve itself. Repairing the faucet valves may require special tools and/or knowledge.

YOUR HOSE CONNECTIONS

WINTERIZING

The convenient water hose connection outside the home is a true asset. It also becomes a liability to a home owner when cold weather comes. In Northern locations, the freeze-proof silcock is standard equipment and in southern regions a standard silcock is familiar. When a vacuum breaker is installed, for protection from backflow, on either of these two hose connections the same danger exists. The vacuum breaker may hold water in the faucet. Water in the faucet that freezes may cause damage or cause it to burst.

☺ Using a pencil eraser, gently toggle the plastic stem in the end of the hose connection vacuum breaker holding it open allowing the water to drain out.

📅 Perform this maintenance every time you winterize your exterior hose connections.

YOUR BACKFLOW PROTECTION

☺ Most people do not know of this common occurrence and are not prepared for its effects. Backflow is when water will flow the opposite direction in the piping system than what is intended. The most common home backflow occurrence is at points where water hoses are connected. Verify that all hose connections (other than washing machine connections) are protected by a vacuum breaker. A vacuum breaker will allow air to be pulled back into the pipes rather than used water, such as water mixed with poison being applied by a hose connected pesticide/fertilizer sprayer. A vacuum breaker will stop backsiphonage of hoses left connected to a valve connection.

Appliances

Your Refrigerator

A refrigerator is not unlike an air-conditioning system. The refrigerator is like your home, and the kitchen where it sits is like the outside world. Just like your home cooling system, the condenser coils must be kept clean. If this is not done, the efficiency is reduced and before long the system no longer cools.

Most refrigerator condensing coils are located in the bottom of the unit. Access may be through the front under the doors or from the back. You may need to pull the refrigerator out into an accessible area before continuing. The cover under the doors is seldom attached with screws. Usually friction tabs are used or lift and pull slots are utilized. Refer to your owner's manual for specific brands.

After gaining access by popping the cover loose, you'll see a huge dust bunny farm. Use your vacuum cleaner with the thin furniture wand and clean this area thoroughly. The coils can be seen with a fan blowing across them and usually a small pan designed to catch condensation below it. In many cases you'll have to remove this pan to vacuum out the coils.

This maintenance item should be performed once each year.

Thoroughly clean the gaskets of the refrigerator and freezer doors. The gaskets around the doors are made from a soft rubber or vinyl material. Use a solution of liquid dish soap and water and a soft brush so damage doesn't occur to these gaskets. Dry the surfaces upon completion and inspect the contact of the gasket to the box. A standard sheet of paper can be placed in the point of contact and should not easily be pulled out. The mating surfaces must be clean.

This maintenance should be performed as needed.

YOUR ICE MAKER

An ice maker in your refrigerator/freezer looks very complicated to the untrained eye. It makes it easier to break it down into its basic components as does most things. The most common malfunction is the control arm is locked in the up position or is not being raised enough to stop the making of ice. The control arm is the arm or lever that extends into the ice storage box. As ice is made the product falls into the storage box and piles up until it pushes the arm up to stop production. If the arm is pushed up and locked, it will stop production. Simply pull it back down to restart production.

ICE MAKER CONNECTION
If your home did not come with an ice maker connection and you're installing the supply line yourself, remember this helpful note. Connect your supply to the hot water line. The water heater acts as a settling tank catching all the impurities that might stop up your new ice maker. This one act will quadruple the life of your ice maker in most cases.

☺ Check to make sure the water line serving your ice maker located on the back of your refrigerator is not kinked or pinched. Verify that the temperature of the freezer is not set below minus four degrees Fahrenheit. Check the 📖 owner's manual on how your model ice maker should be defrosted and cleaned.

📅 Cleaning your ice maker should occur once a year unless you have hard water, then a more rigorous schedule should be adopted.

YOUR CLOTHES DRYER

The most common failure of a clothes dryer and one of the most common causes for home fires is the dryer exhaust being clogged with lint. The clog prevents the correct amount of air movement to allow proper function and the lint can heat up to the point of combustion or allow the clothes within the dryer to heat to the point of combustion. If it takes more than one cycle to dry your clothes, check your dryer exhaust vent.

☺ Pull the dryer out from the wall and ⚡ disconnect the power. Turn off the gas valve behind the dryer if it is a gas unit. A large flexible duct connecting to the dryer exhaust system will normally be found there. It should be connected with clamp bands that can be easily loosened with a slot head screwdriver (some with no tools at all). Remove this flexible duct and vacuum clean inside and out. *If the duct is flammable white plastic, replace it with metal.*

Examine the points of connection on the dryer and at the wall. Remove as much lint from both places. Use caution as the metal duct may have sharp edges. A long flexible lint brush may be used to clean inside ducts. Reconnect the flexible connector duct being careful to prevent any bends and kinks. Turn on the gas if required and plug your dryer back in. Check the duct hood outside. Verify it is not clogged as well. Remove any screens left on by an inexperienced installer as dryer vents must never be screened. Verify the damper is operable, freely swinging out and back closed when released. Watch for accumulation of lint in uncut grass or decorative shrubs near the dryer vent.

This maintenance is typically performed twice a year, more if needed.

YOUR DISHWASHER

A dishwasher is designed to utilize water in a repeated manner. Each cycle, the washer fills up the reservoir in the bottom and pumps it up spraying the dishes over and over with the same water. This water is pumped out and the cycle is repeated with more water in the same reservoir. It is a good design that works well if a person maintains it.

Run the system without dishes or on a load of dishes that will not be harmed by bleach. Pour a half cup of bleach in the bottom of the washer before starting. This will disinfect the entire system. Before loading, always check that large food particles, decals or anything that may clog the drain is removed from the screen in the bottom. Verify the door seal's mating surface is clean, especially at the lower corners of the door. Note that stainless steel will blacken in bleach. 📖 Check your owner's manual to verify bleach will not damage your dish washer.

📅 This maintenance is performed as needed.

FIREPLACES & CHIMNEYS

YOUR FIREPLACE

Several types of fireplaces exist today and it is important
to keep the service up on them. Some fireplaces are for
decoration and others are an important heat source.

GAS FIRED DECORATIVE

The gas fired decorative fireplace will typically have no
exhaust flue. The gas flame is an appliance that uses the
oxygen within the home and releases its exhaust within
the home as well. Be sure to keep the size of this unit as
small as possible. The sizes of these units are measured in
BTU/hour. It should be less than 10,000 BTU/hour.

WOOD BURNING INSERTS

The sheet metal units inserted into a framed wall are
listed appliances that must be maintained per the
manufacturer's service guide. The tag displaying the
manufacturer must be located on or in the front of the
unit. Their product guides are posted on the internet. The
chimney flue is cleaned in the same manner as masonry
chimneys listed below.

WOOD BURNING MASONRY FIREPLACES

Inspect the mortar holding the stones together. If you see
deterioration in this portion of the fireplace, call a mason
before you use the fireplace. "The stones are only as good
as the mortar." In many cases mortar is not properly
mixed and may deteriorate much more rapidly than it
should.

If you notice a white powdery substance forming on the surface of the brick, this could mean that moisture is coming through the brick or stone. The masonry may need to be sealed. Tests show moisture can pass through a brick in twenty seconds. Call a mason to reseal the masonry inside and out.

YOUR CHIMNEY

CLEANING

The most important maintenance on any wood burning fireplace or stove is cleaning the chimney flue. The flue should be cleaned when the creosote is nearing ¼-inch thick.

Measure the flue pipe and order your brush to fit your flue. A proper fit is essential. You also need to know how long your chimney is to have the proper length of handle. Make sure your flue cap is removable. If it is not, you may want to use an experienced chimney sweep. Make sure no power lines are close by.

Open the damper fully. Seal off the fireplace opening with paper and masking tape. This will help to prevent debris from entering the home. Seal it off air tight. *Do not use plastic bags.* Place plastic over carpet and furniture in the work area and on the path outside.

At the top of the chimney, remove the flue cap and push the broom into the flue. Work the brush up and down to knock off the pieces of creosote. Work the entire chimney until it is clean. Inspect the flue liner to verify no damage

47

exists. Use a strong flashlight to verify your work. Replace the chimney cap.

After the dust has settled remove the paper from the fireplace opening (or stove) and sweep or vacuum out the debris. Using a stiff brush, clean the inside of the fire box and on masonry fireplaces clean off the smoke shelf located above the damper. Vacuum out the firebox once more. Use paper bags to remove debris as it will stick to any plastic it comes in contact with and make a mess. Dump all the ashes and creosote into your compost.

Note – Use eye protection and gloves during the cleaning process. The debris produced is abrasive.

Perform this maintenance at least once a year and more on fireplaces used very frequently. Up to four times a year in some places.

Was soll ich werden? Franz Bonn 1888

IRRIGATION SYSTEMS

WATER CONSERVATION & MAINTENANCE

HEADS

The method in which the typical lawn irrigation waters a lawn is most commonly through sprinkler heads. There are several types of sprinkler heads available. The most common are "fixed spray heads" (may or may not be the pop-up design) and "rotary spray heads". It is important to keep the same type and brand in each zone. So replacement of heads should be of the same type and brand. Different types have different flow rates which will prevent an even coverage.

☺ During normal operation make observations of each head and the pattern of spray. If the pattern is hitting a fence of wall or if it sprays over a sidewalk, the head may need to be adjusted, replaced or relocated. If a head is not spraying a typical pattern or is bubbling up with no spray, it is probably stopped up or damaged. Most heads twist lock into place and can be removed without tools or simply screw in. Cleaning a head yourself can save a service call that would cost more than this book.

Watch for wet spots around heads when the rest of the yard is dry. This would indicate a valve is leaking and wasting water. Watch for dry spots in the yard that would indicate incorrect coverage of spray heads. Many "fixed spray heads" can be adjusted with the turn of a screw. They are normally set at quarter circle increments (1/4,

1/2, 3/4, full circle). The adjustment is located in the top of the head.

📅 This maintenance is performed as needed.

TIMER

There is a wide variety of timer/control systems. 📖 Refer to your owner's manual for specific operations and features. When the power goes out, resetting the time is the most common maintenance. Some come with battery backup systems that will require a battery replacement twice a year. To program your unit, consult your local water department for helpful hints for your specific region. 📖 Then use your owner's manual to program the system.

📅 This maintenance is performed as needed and replacement of the backup batteries should occur twice a year.

TESTING BACKFLOW ASSEMBLIES

Your backflow protection is a device that prevents the water outside in the irrigation system or on the ground from being pulled back into the water you and your neighbors drink. The different types of backflow prevention assemblies used are:

Atmospheric Vacuum Breaker (AVB)

Pressure Vacuum Breaker (PVB)

Double Check Assembly (DC)

Reduced Pressure Zone Assembly (RP)

The DC is prohibited in most water jurisdictions because failure can occur without indication. The AVB must not be used where a valve is placed downstream of it. The PVB, DC and RP are testable assemblies. ⊕ *They should be tested by personnel that has been properly trained and in some states must also be licensed.*

☻ Check with your local authority having jurisdiction to verify "Required" intervals of tests. If none are required, most manufacturers recommend at least bi-annual tests. If you have an injection system, your RP (which is required) must be tested at least annually. Never pipe around or bypass a backflow prevention assembly. *The ultimate authority for backflow education is the University of Southern California's Foundation for Cross-Connection Control and Hydraulics Research (http://www.usc.edu/dept/fccchr/).*

WINTERIZING YOUR SYSTEM

YOUR PIPING SYSTEM

In Northern regions irrigation systems are usually built with a Schrader valve to blow out the lines. This valve looks similar to the valve stem on an automobile tire, only slightly larger. Turn off the water supply. Using an air compressor, pressurize your system to 35 to 40 psi. Operate the controller to open each zone and force the water out of the lines through the heads. Maintain the air pressure while performing this action two or three times.

In regions where the freeze line is less than one inch or nonexistent, blowing the lines out is not required.

Winterize before the first freeze of the season.

YOUR BACKFLOW ASSEMBLIES

If your backflow assembly is located above ground (and outside), it should be drained of all water. Opening the test cocks one quarter turn each will allow air to enter the chambers. Even after opening the test cocks, some water may be in the assembly. For individual units, record the brand name and model number. Most of the manufacturers have posted weatherizing instructions for their models. Note that AVB's do not have test ports. PVB's have two test ports. RP's have four test ports.

Winterize before the first freeze of the season.